Hide and Seek

Debbie Witmer
and
Leysan S.

ZZZz

It was a wonderful afternoon for a nap. Bandit was dreaming of bones and treats.

What could possibly go wrong?

I'm so sneaky!

Are you awake?

I am now.

Buzz loves to wake up Bandit. Fun!

Bandit doesn't enjoy it as much as Buzz does.

I'm so happy
you're awake.
Let's play a game.

Let's play
get off of me.

Okay,
Now let's play
something else.

What do you
want to play?

How about
Cops and Robbers?
Nah...
Police

How about Garbage Truck and Evil Trash Bag?
What! No!

How about Pizza King and Lowly Peasant?
Pizza King? Is that a thing?
PIZZA

Secretly, Bandit wonders where Buzz gets all the props for the games.

How about... .
Buzz, please stop!

Bandit suggests they play a game of hide and seek.

No props needed for that one.

Mmm....
I don't know how
to play that.

I can teach you.
I'm a hide and
seek expert!

Bandit tells Buzz that one dog will count with their eyes covered and the other one will hide. Then the first dog needs to find the hidden friend.

That's easy. I can do that.

You get to go hide first. But let's play outside. There's more room to hide.

This will be fun.
Good luck Bandit.
I'll count to 10.
you go hide.

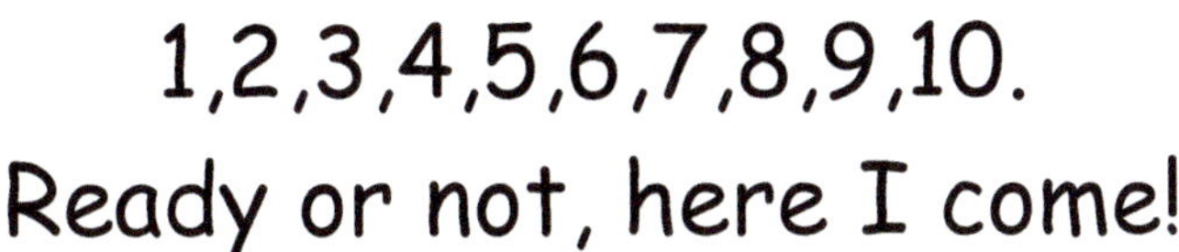

1,2,3,4,5,6,7,8,9,10.
Ready or not, here I come!

Bandit is sure that as a
hide and seek expert, he
will find Buzz right away.

I see him.

Gotcha!
Yikes... .

Oh, excuse me
little rabbit.
I was looking
for Buzz.

Rabbit ears do look a
little bit like
Frenchie ears.
Buzz is not here.
Try the woods.

Even a hide and seek expert
can confuse Frenchie ears
and rabbit ears.

Where could
he be?

That's not a rabbit.
It must be Buzz.
I'll get him this time.

Gotcha!
Yikes... .

Excuse me little fox.
I was looking for
Buzz.
Well, fox ears do look a
little like Frenchie ears.
Buzz is not here.
Did you check the cave?

Even a hide and seek expert can confuse Frenchie ears and rabbit ears.... and fox ears.

I'm not
so sure about
this.
Enter at
your own
risk!

It's so dark in here.
Buzz? Are you here?

Bandit is not sure that playing hide and seek is a good idea anymore.

Oh good.
There are some
Frenchie ears.

Gotcha!

Oh no... . Sorry little bat. I was looking for Buzz.

Hee hee hee hee!

Why are you laughing?
I have never seen a Frenchie hang from the roof of a cave before
What?!?!

Are you okay?
I think so....

Now Bandit is not sure
if he is a hide and seek
expert anymore. He also
believes he may not be a
Frenchie ear expert either.

Signs?
If you want to find Buzz, then just follow the signs.

BUZZ
Buzz
Buzz
Go This Way!
Where did these
signs come from?

You found me Bandit.
Let's have a pizza
party to celebrate!
Finally!
Pizza
Pizza
Pizza
Pizza

I got too much pizza.
It's okay. I met some friends when I was looking for you.
Pizza
Pizza
Pizza
Pizza

Come out. Come out
wherever you are.
It's pizza party time!

Pizza
Pizza
Pizza
Pizza

Before going to sleep, Buzz asked Bandit, "What do you want to play tomorrow?" But Bandit did not answer. He was already asleep.